This is going to be good.

FIND YOUR HAPPY

WRITTEN BY **M.H. CLARK** ~ DESIGNED BY **SARAH FORSTER**

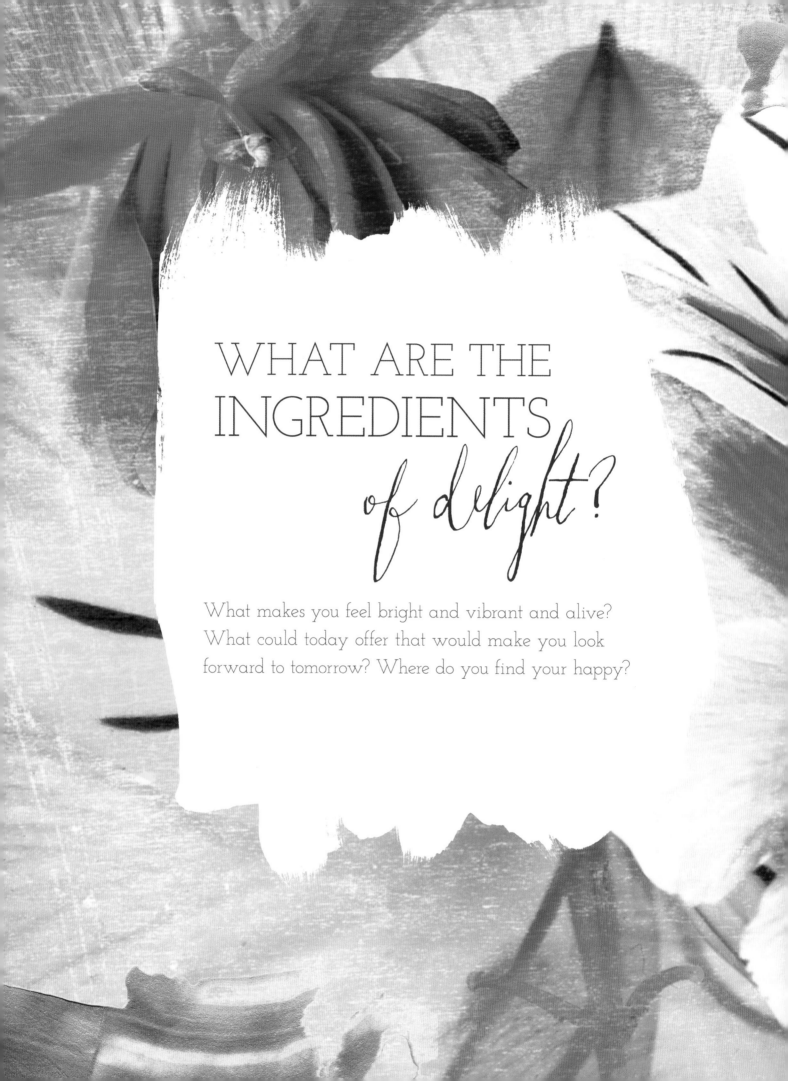

WHAT ARE THE INGREDIENTS *of delight?*

What makes you feel bright and vibrant and alive? What could today offer that would make you look forward to tomorrow? Where do you find your happy?

The answer to that question is yours. It is as unique and completely original as you are, and the answer you give today may not be the same as it will be tomorrow. Happiness is a day by day, hour by hour journey.

The world offers you music and silence, sparkle and shadow, companionship and solitude, oceans and forests and mountains, cities and neighborhoods and someplace where you are really, truly home. The world offers you these gifts every day, and you can decide what you will do with them, how you will make them into a life that is right, a life that is yours, a life where you know just how and where your happiness can be found.

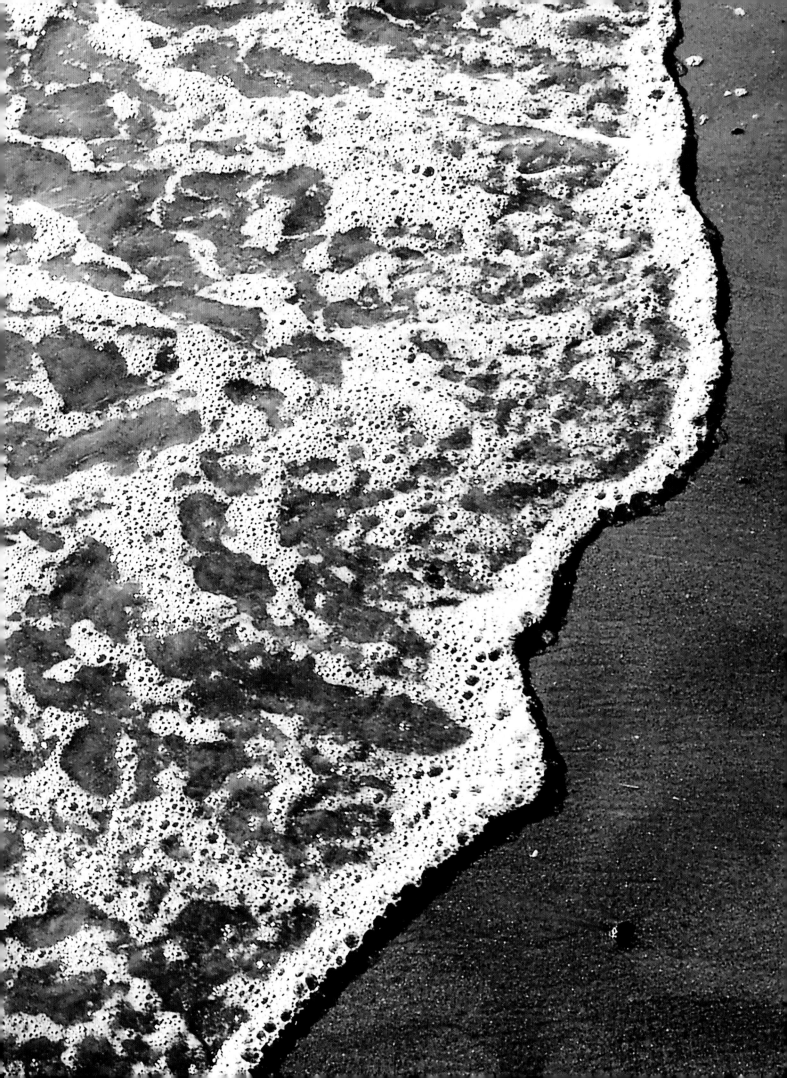

Begin right now.

BEGIN WITH YOU.

BEGIN WITH YOUR FEET ON THE GROUND

AND JOY IN YOUR HEART.

You are here.
And that is good.

Now, everything is possible.

Believe THAT THIS IS
A GOLDEN DAY AND YOU
ARE GOLDEN TOO.

THERE IS NO EDGE
TO YOUR SPIRIT
AND NO LIMIT
TO *your joy.*

Choose this moment.

FIND YOUR HAPPY

TODAY,
LIKE EVERY DAY,
CONTAINS AT LEAST
ONE THING
THAT WILL MAKE YOU
LIGHT UP.
IF YOU HAVEN'T FOUND IT,
BE ON THE LOOKOUT.

And if you have found it, find another.

Follow the spark.

CHASE IT WHERE IT GOES.
LIVE FROM JOY TO JOY,
FROM YES TO *yes.*

There is, in your heart,

A HILL WHERE THE SUN IS SHINING AND
THE DAISIES GROW, ALL DAY, EVERY DAY.

You can go there any time.

SEIZE EVERY SINGLE CHANCE
YOU CAN TO LIVE LOUD AND OPEN
and deliciously free.

Begin with you.

FIND YOUR HAPPY

Your song is sweet and bright and wise and *full,*

AND YOU ARE THE ONLY ONE WHO CAN SING IT.

DECIDE WHAT IT WILL LOOK LIKE
WHEN YOUR HEART IS TRULY HOME.
THEN GO THERE.

CONTENTMENT IS ALWAYS THERE,

RUNNING THROUGH YOU LIKE A RIVER
YOU CAN CHOOSE TO VISIT ANY TIME YOU PLEASE.
SOMETIMES YOU WILL WALK ALONGSIDE IT,
AND SOMETIMES YOU WILL *jumps right in.*

Of course this is your day.

Every day is your day,
and wants to be.

Seek delight.

FIND YOUR HAPPY

This world CONTAINS MORE MIRACLES THAN ANYTHING ELSE, THOUGH THOSE MIRACLES GO BY SIMPLE NAMES: SUNSHINE, BIRD SONG, FREE TIME, FRIENDSHIP, DANCING, LAUGHTER, LOVE.

Right now,
within your reach,
is something
worth celebrating.

THE CHILD IN YOUR HEART WANTS
THE WINDOWS
ROLLED DOWN.
THE CHILD IN YOUR HEART WANTS
TO SING ALONG
WITH THE RADIO.
AND AN ICE CREAM ON THE WAY HOME,

just because.

(the child in your heart is full of good ideas.)

TURN UP THE VOLUME ON
THE GOOD STUFF.

Love what's here.

FIND YOUR HAPPY

YOU HAVE HUNDREDS OF GOOD

BUT ONE OF THE VERY

REASONS TO BE HERE RIGHT NOW,
BEST IS SIMPLY TO *have fun.*

DECIDE, WITH YOUR WHOLE HEART AND YOUR WHOLE MIND, THAT THIS DAY IS MADE TO BE ENJOYED.

Take responsibility for your happiness.

KEEP WHAT IT ASKS TO KEEP
AND CHANGE WHAT IT ASKS TO CHANGE.
TREAT IT WITH SERIOUSNESS,
AND SINCERITY, AND GIVE IT
PLENTY OF TIME TO *play.*

THERE IS A BELL IN YOU
THAT'S FINE-TUNED TO EVERY GOOD THING.

Pay attention to it,
notice what makes it ring.

Look forward.

FIND YOUR HAPPY

MAKE ROOM FOR
MORE—
MORE POSSIBILITY, MORE SPONTANEITY,
MORE DELIGHT,

MORE BOUNDLESS ENERGY,
MORE SWEETNESS,
MORE SPARKLE, MORE
LIGHT.

And return,
AS OFTEN AS YOU CAN,
TO THE THINGS THAT
KEEP YOU WHOLE.

THE PATH YOU'RE ON
THIS VERY MOMENT

is going somewhere good.

BELIEVE THAT
THERE IS STILL MORE
brilliance coming.

Go.

FIND YOUR HAPPY

COMPENDIUM
live inspired

WITH SPECIAL THANKS TO
THE ENTIRE COMPENDIUM FAMILY.

CREDITS:
WRITTEN & COMPILED BY: M.H. CLARK
DESIGNED BY: SARAH FORSTER
EDITED BY: AMELIA RIEDLER
CREATIVE DIRECTION BY: JULIE FLAHIFF

PHOTOGRAPHY CREDITS:

COVER, PAGE 1: MALLOMOI / PHOTOCASE.COM
PAGE 2-3: © LABOKO / DOLLAR PHOTO CLUB, © ALISA / DOLLAR PHOTO CLUB,
    © QUEEN21 / DOLLAR PHOTO CLUB & OLHA KLEIN / CREATIVE MARKET
PAGE 4-5: FLÜGELWESEN / PHOTOCASE.COM
PAGE 8-9: © HELEN RUSHBROOK / STOCKSY UNITED
PAGE 10-11: RUEW1 / PHOTOCASE.COM
PAGE 13: BILDERSOMMER / PHOTOCASE.COM
PAGE 14-15: SUZE / PHOTOCASE.COM
PAGE 18-19: JUDIGRAFIE / PHOTOCASE.COM
PAGE 20-21: SEEPIA.DE / PHOTOCASE.COM
PAGE 23: SIPAPHOTO / PHOTOCASE.COM
PAGE 24-25: WILLMA... / PHOTOCASE.COM
PAGE 26-27: NURMALSO / PHOTOCASE.COM
PAGE 29: PILENS / PHOTOCASE.COM
PAGE 33: YTK / PHOTOCASE.COM
PAGE 34-35: MELLA / PHOTOCASE.COM & SARAH FORSTER
PAGE 38-39: © ALLOY PHOTOGRAPHY / VEER & © QUEEN21 / DOLLAR PHOTO CLUB
PAGE 40-41: THOMAS BARWICK / TAXI / GETTY IMAGES
PAGE 43: CDK / PHOTOCASE.COM
PAGE 44-45: SARAH FORSTER
PAGE 46-47: ESKEMAR / PHOTOCASE.COM
PAGE 50-51: © PILOTL39 / DOLLAR PHOTO CLUB
PAGE 53: ESKEMAR / PHOTOCASE.COM & SARAH FORSTER
PAGE 54-55: © MELANIE DEFAZIO / STOCKSY UNITED
PAGE 56-57: JALA / PHOTOCASE.COM
PAGE 60-61: JORDAN SIEMENS / ICONICA / GETTY IMAGES
PAGE 63: © KUSHNIROV AVRAHAM / DOLLAR PHOTO CLUB
PAGE 64: TACHIKOMA / PHOTOCASE.COM

Library of Congress: 2014943683
ISBN: 978-1-938298-38-7

2nd printing. Printed in China with soy inks.